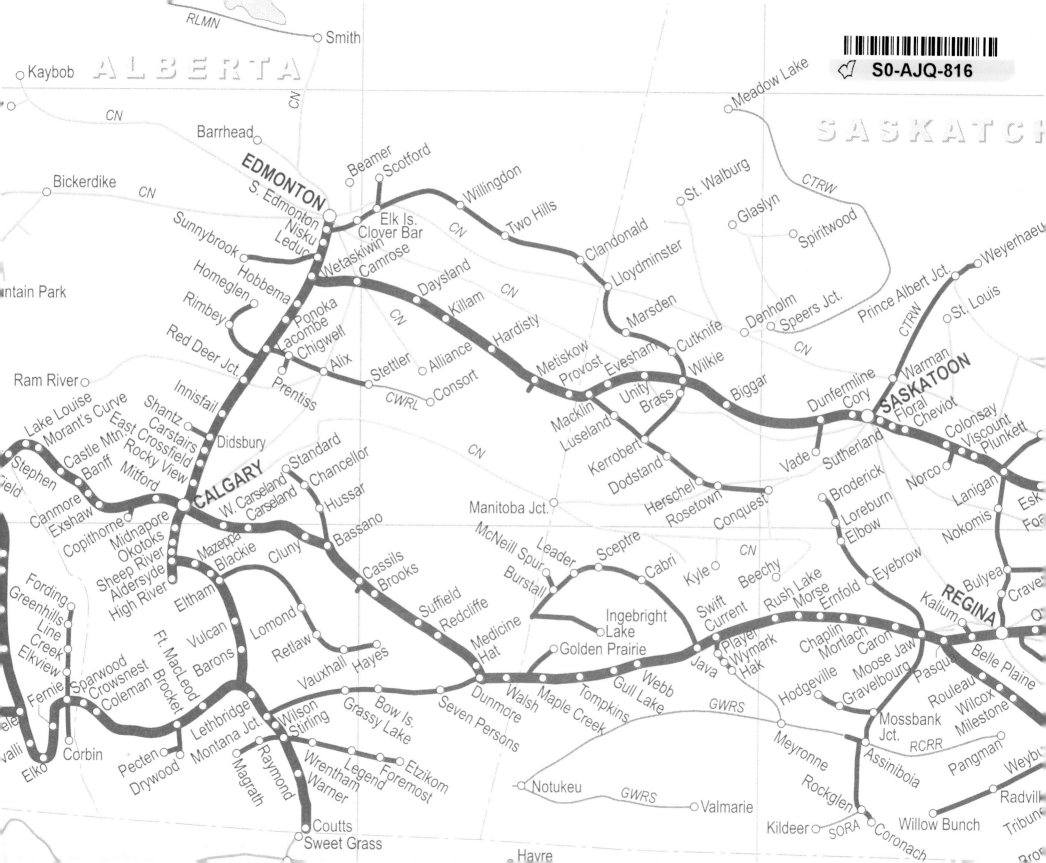

S0-AJQ-816

ROCKY MOUNTAIN

Sunrise

STEAMSCENES

NILS HUXTABLE

© 2009
Published by Steamscenes
2254 Lawson Avenue
West Vancouver, B.C. V7V 2E4
Canada

Distributed in Great Britain by:
Steamscenes UK
Paxton Villa, Bakers Hill
Coleford, Glos. GL16 7QB

Printed in Canada by:
Hemlock Printers Ltd.

ISBN: 978-0-9810812-0-5

Abbreviations:

Alco	American Locomotive Company
AOE	*American Orient Express*
BC Rail	British Columbia Railway
BN	Burlington Northern
BNSF	Burlington Northern Santa Fe
CEFX	The CIT Group/Capital Finance Inc.
CLC-FM	Canadian Locomotive Company/Fairbanks-Morse
CN/CNR	Canadian National/Canadian National Railways
CP/CPR	CP Rail/Canadian Pacific Railways
DPU	Distributed Power Unit
GE	General Electric
GM	General Motors
GN	Great Northern
LMX	GE-owned locomotives leased to BN on a power-by-the-hour basis
MLW	Montreal Locomotive Works
NAR	Northern Alberta Railways
RM	*Rocky Moutaineer*
SRY	Southern Railway of B.C.
UP	Union Pacific RR

Cover Design and Layout:
Ray Cherniak, Nils Huxtable, Randy Kandt and Peter Madliger

Endpapers:
Clarke Sutphin

Contributing Photographers:
Roger Burrows, Ray Cherniak, Donald Duke,
Doug Cummings, Kevin Dunk, Tom Ellis, Bob Gordon,
Bob Hunter, Nils Huxtable, Brian Jennison, John Leopard,
Mo Morrison, Gary Miller, Ros Miller, Mo Morrison,
Jeff Robertson, James Speaker, Ken Storey and
Richard Yaremko

Acknowledgements:
Special thanks to the railroad employees and preservationists
who helped make this book possible.

Front Cover:
CPR H1b 4-6-4 No. 2816 *Empress* accelerates through Morant's
Curve. 9/01 (Ken Storey)

Page One:
The *Royal Canadian Pacific* departs Gap, Alberta for Calgary.
7/03

Page Two:
Four AC4400CWs complete the 14.6-mile ascent from Field,
B.C. to Divide, Alberta. 9/02

Title page:
Sara and No. 2816 at Sicamous, B.C.
7/06 (Three photos: Nils Huxtable)

ROCKY MOUNTAIN SUNRISE

By Nils Huxtable

East of Lake Louise, Alberta, the Canadian Pacific Railway and the Bow River come together. As you look to the west from Highway 1A, the Rockies dominate the scene: Mount Lefroy, Mount Aberdeen, Saddle and Fairview Mountains, Mount White and Mount Niblock. To the casual visitor, it matters little whether a train passes. Freights are infrequent, and most tourists have better things to do than wait for an empty grain extra or a double-stack.

Train photographers, however, seem content to spend hours doing just that. To them, the time of day, season of the year and clarity of light assume an importance incomprehensible to the average observer. Most railway enthusiasts agree that autumn and winter mornings, blessed with clear skies and low light, are best. There's nothing like a Rocky Mountain sunrise.

Nicholas Morant loved winter. Accompanied by his 4x5 and 5x7 cameras, he preferred the cold, still, glistening conditions left by a fall of snow. The fewer the hours of illumination, the more precious they were.

For the better part of 50 years, Morant worked as the CPR's official photographer. Following the removal of some trees, he found a location on the Laggan Subdivision between Calgary and Field. To Morant, the new vista included everything he valued most in a railway picture: an s-curve, a river, and above all, the Rockies.

Left:
In 1998, CP rescued No. 2816 from the Steamtown National Historic Site in Scranton, Pennsylvania. A three-year re-fit included a new cab, overhauled boiler, new driver tyres and conversion to oil firing. A movie run at Morant's Curve was the highlight of the Hudson's 5-Day trek from Vancouver to Calgary. 9/01 (Ken Storey)

Above:
Reflecting the 21st Century boom in container traffic from the Far East, two AC4400CWs pass the same location. 5/06 (Nils Huxtable)

Above:
Westbound, four GEs observe a 40-mph speed restriction through the curve.

Right:
Formed as a Crown Corporation in January 1977 to take over CN and CP passenger services, VIA Rail assumed responsibility for *The Canadian* on October 29, 1978. Nick Morant recorded the final run of the eastbound train at this spot on January 15, 1990.
1/86

Pages 10-11:
Just west of Ashcroft, B.C. two railroads and the Thompson River share Black Canyon. The CPR arrived in 1885, the Canadian Northern Pacific Railway, 30 years later. Although the CNP's last spike was driven a few miles to the west, at Basque, on January 23, 1915, the collapse of Black Canyon Tunnel postponed the official opening of the line by six months. A westbound sulphur train snakes out of Cornwall Tunnel.
10/08 (Three photos: Nils Huxtable)

Morant's masterpiece depicts, not steam, but the CPR's stainless-steel domeliner. The Bow River lies partly hidden, encrusted with ice and mantled by snowdust. First published on the cover of *The Spanner*, the railroad's employee magazine, the same illustration has re-appeared many times. Indeed, the Rockies and *The Canadian* seemed made for each other.

Morant exposed so much film at MP 113.0 that the CPR's Publicity Department began referring to it as 'Morant's Corner'. Then, in *Rails in the Northwest*, author Ronald C. Hill first coined the phrase 'Morant's Curve'.

Since then, the curve has become a legend. As a must-see place of railway interest, it ranks alongside the Cisco bridges, the Spiral Tunnels, Pavilion, the Kettle Valley Railway, Crowsnest Pass or Rocky Mountain House. As a photographic jewel, it knows no equal. River and railway lead the eye to the headlight of an eastbound train, seemingly appearing from nowhere. Paradoxically, the Rockies themselves, while enhancing the picture, diminish the train's significance. Railway photographers revere Morant's Curve. No Canadian train book would be complete without it.

Rocky Mountain Sunrise celebrates railroads in the Canadian West; its mountains, valleys, canyons, prairies, rivers, lakes, forests – and people. What better place to begin than Morant's Curve, in full view of what the Stoney First Nations call "the Shining Mountains"?

Far Left:
One of the largest modern-day gatherings of steam power in North America, Steam-expo, held in Vancouver during May 1986, featured 21 locomotives. CPR G5a 4-6-2 No. 1201 (Angus Shops, 1944) and CNR H-6-g 4-6-0 No. 1392 (MLW, 1913) pose in CN's Main yard.

Left:
Returning to Ottawa, No. 1201 is being readied at Field, B.C. for the 2.2% ascent of Kicking Horse Pass. Named after American businessman Cyrus W. Field, the location was a helper/pusher base in steam days. 7/86 (Both: Nils Huxtable)

Above:
Jointly owned by the CPR and CNR after 1929, the Northern Alberta Railways became part of CN's Mountain Region in 1981. The Smoky and Grande Prairie Subs serve the Peace River grain district. At Sexsmith, Alberta, Train No. 31 is led by GP9 No. 201 *McLennan*. 6/74 (Richard Yaremko)

Right:
Alberta RailNet operated 364 miles of ex-NAR trackage from 1999 until 2006, when CN reacquired it. Crossing the Berland River south of Sexsmith with Train No. 459, the daily Grande Cache to Swan Landing turn, are four of ARN's second-hand GE C30-7s. 10/99 (Jeff Robertson)

Left:
Eastbound grain empties leave the Lower Spiral Tunnel. Unique to North America, the CPR's Spiral Tunnels, built in 1907-09 at a cost of $ 1,500,000, reduced the ruling grade between Field and Hector, B.C. from 4.5% to 2.2%. 7/04 (Nils Huxtable)

Above:
Rocky Mountain sunset. A westbound stack train begins the descent of Kicking Horse Pass. At an elevation of 5,332 feet, this is the highest point on the CPR, marking both the Continental Divide and the boundary between Banff and Yoho National Parks. 9/01 (Ken Storey)

The Kamloops Heritage Railway's ex-CNR M-3-d 2-8-0 spent most of its working life on the Prairies and Vancouver Island. Retired in 1958 and displayed at the city's Riverside Park, No. 2141 was steamed after eight years of restoration. The 1912-built Consolidation re-starts its train on the South Thompson River bridge, which included a single swing span to allow the steamboat *Sue Ann* to pass. 7/06 (Nils Huxtable)

Five of CNR's 56 H-6-g 4-6-0s remained on the roster until 1961. No. 1392 joined the Alberta Pioneer Railway's collection after being displayed at the Edmonton Exhibition grounds for 12 years. A typical duty for this Ten-Wheeler was the thrice-weekly Neepawa Local, covering the 60 miles between Brandon, Manitoba and Neepawa in both directions. 5/86 (Nils Huxtable)

Right:
Clocking 462.4 miles on the days it ran to Prince George, the *Cariboo Prospector* provided one of the longest Budd car rides on the continent. Grinding up the 2.2% through the Cheakamus Canyon, Train No.1 slows for the bridge (Mile 55.43) near Swift, B.C. Replacing a 606.7-ft long timber trestle in 1927, this structure, consisting of six deck plate girder spans resting on concrete piers and abutments, is 470 feet long. 5/88

Far Right:
After 86 years, passenger service ended on November 1, 2002. Thereafter, only the *Whistler Mountaineer* and an occasional CN executive special operated over the Squamish Sub. One such business train returns to North Vancouver from Whistler. 6/02 (Both: Nils Huxtable)

Right:
The privately owned B.C. Electric Railway became the provincially-owned B.C. Hydro Railway in 1962. Twenty-six years later, the Washington Group purchased the line and changed the name to the Southern Railway of B.C. (SRY). It serves communities along the 63 miles between New Westminster and Chilliwack, as well as catering to local industries. Two SD38-2s drop down Kennedy Hill with a few cars retrieved from a derailment. 10/06

Far Right:
Burgeoning coal traffic from the Crowsnest mines to the Roberts Bank marine terminal has transformed the Golden-Fort Steele section of the 143-mile Windermere Subdivision into a busy thoroughfare. As many as six 14,000-ton trains ply the line each day. Empties pass the bluffs at Radium, B.C. 9/07 (Both: Nils Huxtable)

Left:
In charge of a grain extra, two 4300-hp SD90MACs take advantage of the 5.5-mile Stephen Revision, the new westbound main (completed in 1981) between Lake Louise and Divide, which reduced the grade from 1.9 to 1.0 percent. 9/01

Above:
When this picture was taken, the CP-CN joint-running agreement was still being discussed. Diverted to CN rails because of track repairs, an eastbound CP manifest clatters over Fraser River bridge No. 10 west of Lytton, B.C. Consisting of four deck plate girder and three deck truss spans, the 1914-built structure is 869 feet long and 148 feet high. Sixty-one of these locomotives arrived in 1998 and 1999. 8/99 (Both: Nils Huxtable)

Right:
An overall view from the Lions Gate suspension bridge of CN's (ex-BC Rail) North Vancouver yard; MP 2.0 of the Squamish Subdivision. Local industries include Vancouver Wharves, as well as trans-loading facilities for wood chips and sulphur. 11/06

Far Right:
Less than a quarter of a mile to the west, a work train powered by a Burro crane trundles onto the Capilano River bridge after replacing ties. The railway to Squamish was completed on June 10, 1956 and officially opened on August 27 of that year. 11/06 (Both: Nils Huxtable)

Completed in 1970, the lift bridge over Burrard Inlet takes the weight of a grain shuttle from CN's Lynn Creek yard, on the North Shore Industrial line, the end of CN's Thornton Sub. 10/06 (Nils Huxtable)

The Grand Trunk Pacific Railway
completed its 720-mile line from Jasper
to Prince Rupert in 1914. Successor
CNR added 40 miles between Terrace and
Kitimat. In Kitsellas Canyon, east of Terrace,
B.C., engineers had to blast four bores
similar to the Kettle Valley Railway's
Quintette tunnels. A safety cab-equipped
SD40-2 leads the lash-up of Train No. 457
bound for Kitimat. 8/97 (Jeff Robertson)

Left:
At Matsqui Prairie, B.C. CN's Yale Sub joins and crosses CP's Mission Sub, then makes another connection with CP's Page Sub (used by eastbounds) – all in the space of two miles. Destined for the elevators of North Vancouver, a CP grain extra closes in on the diamond immediately west of Matsqui Junction. 8/06 (Nils Huxtable)

Above:
CN Train No. 101, with containers for the Roberts Bank superport. An early snowfall with chilling winds in this exposed part of the Fraser Valley sometimes rivals the extreme conditions of the true Prairies. 11/06 (Ken Storey)

Above:
CN Train No. 315, a Winnipeg-Calgary overflow job, rolls through the Alberta badlands near Rosebud, on the Drumheller Sub, which extends 131.9 miles from Hanna to Sarcee yard. 2/02 (Ros Miller)

Right:
A westbound manifest emerges from the 186-ft tunnel at MP 120.0 of the Ashcroft Subdivision, onto Nine Mile Creek (or Ainslee Creek) viaduct (303 feet long, 139 feet high), 5.5 miles east of Boston Bar, B.C. Subject to rockslides, this section of railroad, difficult to build and costly to maintain, is sometimes referred to as "Avalanche Alley". 11/06 (Nils Huxtable)

Right:
The *Royal Canadian Pacific* west of Cathe-dral, B.C. The portal's construction date coincides with the completion of the Spiral Tunnels. When the Trans-Canada Highway was built nearby, the CPR decided against "daylighting" this short bore through a shoulder of rock. 9/02

Far Right:
Upgraded to FP9 standards, the train's earlier motive power came from Nebkota Railway in 1998. With a business train, FP7u No. 1400 and F9B No. 1900 are travelling east along Kamloops Lake, B.C., between Savona and Old Munro. Aside from special movements, CPR passenger trains usually passed this scenic highlight in darkness. 9/99 (Both: Nils Huxtable)

Right:
Viewed from the Trans-Canada Highway overpass, seven CP SD40-2s ease down the 2.2% grade through Yoho, half-way between the Upper and Lower Spiral Tunnels: 'Yoho' is a Cree word meaning 'awe' or 'astonishment'. 4/87 (Nils Huxtable)

Far Right:
Completion of the Connaught Tunnel in 1916 solved the worst of the CPR's weather problems trains in Rogers Pass, where snowfalls average 50 feet. Based at Revelstoke, B.C., wedge plows equipped with air-operated wings and retractable nose plates clear the tracks after a storm. At Glacier, the train crew spreads the yard while the section crew cleans the switch points. 2/99 (Jeff Robertson)

Left:
With a large yard and the major diesel maintenance facility for the Kootenay and Kettle Valley Divisions, Nelson, B.C. was still a busy place in 1968. Closure of the Boundary Sub west of Castlegar (69.1 miles) and the Slocan Lake route in 1988 reduced the city's importance as a railway centre. In the foreground, an MLW S-4 assembles a train for Cranbrook. The two left-hand tracks were for car cleaning. 10/68

Above:
The CPR ordered 28 of the 165 Fairbanks-Morse/CLC cab units produced. They were advertised as 'The Consolidation Line'; hence the name 'C-Liner'. CPA16-4 No. 4066 and H16-44 roadswitchers depart with the *Trail Hotshot*. No. 8555 was one of two H16-44s never modified to run short-hood forward. The high-sided yellow ore cars are conveying lead and zinc concentrates from Pine Point, N.W.T. to Cominco's smelter in Trail. 10/68 (Both: Bob Gordon)

VIA Train No. 1, the *Canadian*, stands ready for departure at Revelstoke, B.C. The CPR's 1953 order for 173 Budd-built stainless steel passenger cars included a group of 18 dome-observation sleepers like this one, named after Canada's National and Provincial Parks. Each car included three bedrooms, one drawing room, a 24-seat dome, a 13-seat buffet and a 12-seat observation end. 12/86 (Brian Jennison)

On the point of Train No. 2, former CN FP9 No. 6506, dating from 1954, sends up a geyser from its steam generator after being refuelled. VIA owned more FP7s, FP9s and F9Bs than any other company. From CN and CP, the Crown Corporation purchased 148 locomotives; 1,265 passenger cars; 86 RDCs and 27 Turbo Train cars. 9/84 (Kevin Dunk)

Far Left:
In 1887, the CPR extended its main line 13 miles west along Burrard Inlet from its original Port Moody terminus to a new facility on Coal Harbour. A Vancouver-Coquitlam transfer leaves Renfrew. CN's new Second Narrows bridge, then under construction, replaced the road/rail structure in 1970.1/68

Left:
Even though *The Canadian* got priority, there weren't always enough F-units to cover the service. GP9s sometimes had to fill in, spoiling the streamliner's continuity. Equipped with icicle breakers and Pyle Gyralite (safety features added for passenger train assignments) two FP7s and a GP9 power through Yoho.
12/70 (Both: Bob Gordon)

CP Rail

Right:
In 1979, a new second main line eased the grade for westbounds over Notch Hill, west of Tappen, B.C., from 1.9 to 1.0 percent. Now called the North Track, the 11-mile revision features this six-degree horseshoe curve being taken by a 'red barn' SD40F-2 and three SD40-2s. Notch Hill was the name of the gap through the Shuswap Highlands. 7/93 (Tom Ellis)

Far Right:
A 14,000-ton Sparwood-Roberts Bank coal train erupts from the west portal of Mount Shaughnessy Tunnel. Completed in 1988, the mile-long bore forms part of a 20-mile second main line laid on a 1.0% grade to increase capacity and eliminate the need for manned helpers based at Rogers. 9/94 (Ken Storey)

Right:
Beginning its eastbound trek over CP
tracks, CN Train No. 102 takes advantage
of the CP-CN joint-running agreement as it
approaches the interlocked drawbridge over
the Fraser River at Riverside, B.C.
8/06 (Nils Huxtable)

Far Right:
VIA, Amtrak, CN and BNSF all use the
former GN route between New Westminster
and CN Junction, completed in 1904. F7A
No. 9042 leads two SD40s along GN Cut.
Crews preferred a 'covered wagon' as the
lead unit because it afforded better protec-
tion. Between 1972 and 1974, CN rebuilt
30 F7As, prolonging their lives another 15
years. 4/68 (Bob Gordon)

Above:
Until 1958, the B.C. Electric Railway operated the last vestiges of an interurban service that had once extended from downtown Vancouver to Chilliwack and Steveston. A two-car local enters Old Marpole. The new Oak Street bridge doomed these trains. (Donald Duke)

Right:
BC Rail's 82-mile Tumbler Sub electrics met a similar fate. Completed in 1984, the 50 Kv-electrified 82-mile branch was mothballed just 16 years later, and six of its seven 6000-hp GF6C locomotives were scrapped. Near Whitford, just east of 5.6-mile Table Tunnel, this 98-car train of empties will devour nearly 10,000 tons at the Teck Loadout, for shipment to Japan. The line was de-electrified on October 1, 2000. 9/85 (Nils Huxtable)

Two *Super Continentals* meet east of Jasper, where the westbound train has taken the siding. In response to increased ridership in the 1960s, CN purchased surplus Pullman-Standard full-length domes and 'Skytop Lounge' observation cars from the Milwaukee Road, which had truncated its *Olympian Hiawatha*. Use of the domes continued under VIA, lasting until the *Super's* demise. 2/81 (Bob Gordon)

The conductor boards a CP special from Vancouver to Abbotsford via the Mission Sub. 6/73 (Bob Gordon)

Right:
Crossing the Continental Divide at Summit Lake, these SD40-2s are in full dynamics for the 2.2% descent of Kicking Horse Pass, so-named after a packhorse kicked explorer James Hector. 9/87

Far Right:
West of Revelstoke, the CPR climbs through the Gold Range of the Monashee Mountains over the 1,831-foot summit of Eagle Pass. Finished in 1907, the 1.5-mile Clanwilliam Diversion takes trains through three short tunnels. With a robot car controlling the mid-train helper locomotives or 'slaves', this train of coal empties makes light work of the 1.1% grade. 9/85

Pages 54-55:
Named after Lord Revelstoke, an English financier whose company supported the CPR during its construction, this important division point is busy with coal trains, grain extras and double-stacks. As a westbound waits on the main track, a conductor goes on duty. 10/08 (Three photos: Nils Huxtable)

Far Left:
Following a night of heavy rain, the community of Savona, B.C. (originally, Savona's Ferry) awakens to the arrival of Manifest Train No. 471, Calgary-Coquitlam. Work to extend the 140-car siding is underway, and the engineer must observe a temporary speed restriction. 9/05

Left:
By contrast, a broken rail has caused the slow progress of this train. Four SD40-2s manage to bring forward a few cars of their marooned eastbound near Johnston Creek, Alberta. Named Castle Mountain by James Hector of the Palliser Expedition, its looming ramparts were re-christened Mount Eisenhower by then-Prime Minister MacKenzie-King in 1946. It reverted to its original name in 1979. 9/85 (Both: Nils Huxtable)

Far Left:
CP and CN ceded operation of 157 passenger trains over 15,389 route miles to VIA
Rail. Disposing of most CN equipment, VIA
retained the ex-CP Budd cars. Between
1990 and 1993, the fleet was remanufactured. Near Hatzic, B.C., No. 2 accelerates
after stopping at Mission.
8/06 (Ken Storey)

Left:
A passenger in one of the train's former
CP 'Skyline' domes seems oblivious to the
attractions of CN's Yellowhead Route near
Blue River, B.C. 7/05 (Nils Huxtable)

Left:
Before the boom in freight traffic along the BN (now BNSF) Brownsville, B.C.-Seattle corridor, trains were scarce. Two SD40-2s suffice for southbound Train No. 635, clattering over Mud Bay trestle, between Colebrook and White Rock. 2/85 (Nils Huxtable)

Above:
In the heyday of GN streamliners, the traveller could choose among four *Pacific Internationals*. Because of customs regulations, No. 517, Amtrak's southbound *Cascade*, will not stop in New Westminster, as GN's trains once did. The Braid signal gantry has since been dismantled to make way for additional track at CP Junction. 12/04 (Ken Storey)

Right:
'Royal Hudsons' headed passenger runs between Revelstoke and Vancouver until dieselization in 1954. Fifty-eight years later, last of the original 4-6-4s, H1b No. 2816, pulls out of the yard with a special from Calgary to Coquitlam, B.C.
10/08

Far Right:
In need of replacement power for the *Royal Canadian Pacific,* the CPR acquired two former VIA/CN FP7s, which were rebuilt to GP38-2 specifications. Approaching Cherry Creek, B.C., an eastbound *RCP* takes advantage of new (2007) double track along Kamloops Lake. 10/08 (Both: Nils Huxtable)

Far Left:
CP Train No. 984 descends Crowsnest Pass between Sentinel and Coleman, Alberta; 5.3 miles east of the 4,451-ft summit. The Crowsnest Subdivision runs 101 miles to Lethbridge. In the middle distance, the Jefferson Lake Petrochemicals plant seems dwarfed by the Sentinel Range.
9/96 (Kevin Dunk)

Left:
Before completion of the second main line over Rogers Pass, all trains used Stoney Creek bridge. The CPR's most imposing structure, it consists of a steel arch with a span of 336 feet. In 1929, strengthening arches were added. The bridge is 484 feet long, rising 325 feet above the creek, which flows from the slopes of Mt. Shaughnessy.
4/85 (Nils Huxtable)

Right:
The CPR named many of the sidings on its transcontinental main line after persons involved in its construction. Such a place is Moberly, 7.1 miles west of Golden, B.C. Walter Moberly made preliminary surveys for the Mountain Division and discovered Eagle Pass in 1865. A westbound train holds for a meet with VIA's *Canadian.* 12/88 (Kevin Dunk)

Far Right:
"CP 9651 East – clear to Mission West", calls the engineer of Train No. 470. Already on duty for four hours, the crew will soon be giving the dispatcher their five-hour relief notice, since an on-time arrival at the North Bend crew-change point is doubtful. 11/06 (Ken Storey)

Left:
Having passed Dinosaur Junction, where CN makes a connection with the Central Western Railway, Train No. 115 twists through Fox Coulee, near Drumheller, Alberta. A night operation, the train should have arrived in Calgary's Sarcee yard by this time. 5/05 (Ros Miller)

Above:
Discontinued in 2006, the *American Orient Express* explored routes on schedules unfamiliar to most VIA Rail passengers. This eastbound *AOE* has just met a coal train at Louis Creek, on the south bank of the North Thompson River. Passenger-geared GP40-2L(W)s and a VIA F40PH gather speed through Barriere, an area devastated by fire the following summer. 8/02 (Nils Huxtable)

VIA's westbound *Canadian* pauses at Banff's 1910-built station, where many tour trains stopped overnight until the 1960s. The site of the CPR's first hotel (1887), Banff was named after the Scottish birthplace of a CPR director. Rising in the distance are Mounts Inglismaldie and Girouard.
1/85 (Nils Huxtable)

Painted in VIA's transition scheme, nose lettered in red, this former CPR FP9 featured in a Woodward's photo shoot. VIA chose a similar illustration, including two collegiate models, for the cover of its timetable. Built between 1916 and 1919, Vancouver's CNR terminus was renamed Pacific Central. During the summer of 1986, crowds of visitors passed through these doors to see Vancouver's Expo. 6/86 (Ray Cherniak)

Above:
CPR surveyors selected the Bow River Valley as the best route through the Rockies. In ten weeks, tracks were laid between Mount Rundle and Banff; 81.9 miles. The Three Sisters and Mount Rundle tower above a westbound manifest threading Canmore, Alberta. Today a tourist resort catering to park visitors, Canmore was a CPR division point until 1899. 1/85. (Nils Huxtable)

Right:
In 1998, CP changed the livery of its locomotives from 'Action Red' with the multi-mark logo to a Soo Line wine red and gold with a beaver emblem. Train No. 198 rides above an ice-encrusted Bow River near Seebe, east of Exshaw, Alberta; MP51.8 of the Laggan Sub. It's -34° Celsius. 1/04 (Gary Miller)

With less than a year to go before Alberta RailNet takes control north of Swan Landing, CN Train No. 458, Jasper-Winniandy, shakes the spans of Mason Creek trestle on the Grande Cache South Sub. 9/98 (Jeff Robertson)

CN's E9ARs in their new (July 2004) guise.
Arriving from the west, a three-car business
train slows for North Bend, B.C. Located
on the west bank of the Fraser River, North
Bend is a division point for CP's Thompson
and Cascade Subdivisions.
7/04 (Nils Huxtable)

Above:
By 1994, CN's surviving GP9s had been remanufactured for local service and renumbered. Nos. 7067 and No. 7055 are ready to depart for Thornton Yard with the Chilliwack turn. 10/01

Right:
Amalgamated in 1922, the CNR in Western Canada was formed of the 720-mile Grand Trunk Pacific from Jasper to Prince Rupert and the 529-mile Canadian Northern from Lucerne to Port Mann. Now known as CN's North Line and Yellowhead Route respectively, the lines divide at Red Pass Junction. Near Mile 8.5 of the Albreda Subdivision is Geikie, Alberta, in the Miette River Canyon. An SD70M-powered stack train speeds toward Jasper. 6/04

Pages 96-97:
Continuing the 4000-series allotted to 35 FP7s added to the roster in 1951-53, the *Royal Canadian Pacific's* twins became Nos. 4106 and 4107. East of Spences Bridge, B.C., a shippers' special returns to Calgary. 10/08 (Three photos: Nils Huxtable)

Above:
A work train at Azouzetta, on BC Rails's Chetwynd Sub. B39-8E No. 3901 was one of two rebuilt in 1988, from wrecked LMX units. 6/04

Right:
As early as 1978 passenger service was said to be losing a million dollars annually. By October 2002, the B.C. government had decided to get rid of its provincial railway – Budd cars included. Built with more powerful engines and a redesigned front end, the RDCs were fitted with Path-finder headlights and Swanson airhorns. Maximum speed was 90 mph. Train No. 1 purrs away from Garibaldi. 10/02 (Both: Nils Huxtable)

Left:
Last vestige of the Kettle Valley Railway, the Princeton Subdivision – the CPR's longest – extended 190.1 miles. Twenty-four carloads per month from the Weyerhauser mills in Okanagan Falls and Princeton were not enough to cover operating costs, so CP abandoned the line on May 12, 1989. South of Dot, B.C., a train of empties treads past the smoking remains of some burnt ties and onto Bridge No. 5 over the Nicola River. 2/88 (Bob Hunter)

Above:
Not far from the same location, the weekday Merritt-Spences Bridge wayfreight conveys empty ballast hoppers and finished lumber. When washouts closed the Coquihalla in 1959, CP diverted traffic via the Princeton Sub. In more prosperous times, this business included not only lumber, but perishable fruit, copper and coal. 9/87 (Nils Huxtable)

Right:
In 1999-2001, CP leased 40 4300-hp SD90MACs and 25 AC4400CWs. Used mainly on run-through potash trains between Lethbridge, Alberta and Portland, Oregon, the DPU-equipped GMs also appeared on merchandise trains and executive specials. Two CEFXs depart Fort Steele, B.C. 10/01 (Tom Ellis)

Far Right:
Lasting as a through route for only 43 years, the CPR's 962-mile secondary main line across southern Alberta and B.C. once saw such passenger accommodations as the *Kootenay Central Mixed*, the *Kettle Valley Express* and the longest Budd RDC run on the continent. Today, only the passage of the luxurious *Royal Canadian Pacific* or a business train interrupts the flow of potash, grain, merchandise and coal. On the ascent from Pincher Creek, Alberta, a Portland-Minneapolis shippers' special leaves the Rockies in the care of an early winter storm. 11/05 (Ros Miller)

Right:
Introduced in 1990, the Great Canadian Railtour Company's *Rocky Mountaineer* travels the CN and CP transcontinental main lines. At Kamloops, the eastbound train divides. Returning to Vancouver from Jasper and Calgary, the combined consists past Seddall, B.C., where the Thompson River rapids begin. Author Fred W. Frailey described this landscape as "suggestive of the surface of the moon". 9/01

Far Right:
Standard power for the *RM's* ex-CN coaches and new dome cars has ranged from former Santa Fe B36-7s to ex-CSX GP40-2s and ex-CN GP40-2L(W)s. The westbound train speeds through Exshaw, Alberta, another favourite area for Nick Morant. An opening in the Rockies carved by the Bow River, "The Gap" enabled surveyors to map out a route for the CPR main line. 9/01 (Both: Nils Huxtable)

Far Left:
Despite implementation of the CP-CN joint-running agreement, trains occasionally revert to traditional operating practice. Two GEs burst out of the fourth and longest (544 feet) of four rock bores east of Yale. At the time of the construction, blasting these tunnels with nitro-glycerine took 18 months. 10/97 (Bob Gordon)

Left:
To symbolize its cross-border business, CP briefly adopted a dual-flag logo. Two AC4400CWs and an SD40-2 cross Skuzzy Creek bridge, a 131-ft deck truss span 5.5 miles west of North Bend, B.C. The *Skuzzy* was a steamboat used to ferry materials along Kamloops Lake during the CPR's construction. 5/00 (Jeff Robertson)

Last operator of Climax-type locomotives in North America, the Hillcrest Lumber Company shut down in August 1968. At the Mesachie Lake Mill are Nos. 9 (in steam) and 10 (in reserve). No. 9 found a new home at the B.C. Forest Discovery Centre in Duncan, No. 10 with the Mount Rainier Scenic Railroad at Mineral, Washington. 8/66 (Doug Commings)

Another Vancouver Island lumber concern, MacMillan Bloedel, relied on steam through 1969. The company's 1929-built 2-8-2ST began hauling tourist trains from Port Alberni 73 years later. The fireman adjusts the firing valve. 7/03 (Nils Huxtable)

Left:
Following its inauguration, the *Royal Canadian Pacific* made several end-of-year trips from Calgary, turning either at Field or Lake Louise. With Partridge siding, Yoho and the Spiral Tunnels behind it, an eastbound *RCP* roars toward Hector, B.C. 1/03 (Gary Miller)

Above:
VIA Train No. 2, the *Canadian,* enters the snowshed (since replaced by a snow fence) on the approach to Mount Stephen Tunnel. At the other end of the bore, a second snowshed was demolished by a rockslide in 1977. 12/88 (Kevin Dunk)

Page 112:
A last glimpse of Morant's Curve. No. 2816 steams home to Calgary. 5/06 (Nils Huxtable)